IMAGES
of America

DETROIT'S BELLE ISLE

ISLAND PARK GEM

IMAGES of America

DETROIT'S BELLE ISLE

ISLAND PARK GEM

Michael Rodriguez and Thomas Featherstone

ARCADIA
PUBLISHING

Published by Arcadia Publishing
Charleston, South Carolina

Printed in the United States of America

Library of Congress Catalog Card Number: 2002116778

For all general information contact Arcadia Publishing at:
Telephone 843-853-2070
Fax 843-853-0044
E-mail sales@arcadiapublishing.com
For customer service and orders:
Toll-Free 1-888-313-2665

Visit us on the Internet at www.arcadiapublishing.com

CONTENTS

ACKNOWLEDGMENTS

The authors wish to thank David Poremba and Dawn Eurich of the Burton Historical Collection at the Detroit Public Library, Patience Nauta of the Detroit Historical Museums, John Polacsek of the Dossin Great Lakes Museum, and the staff at the library of Michigan State University—including Kathleen Weessies and Stephanie Bour, and especially Jane Arnold. Warmest thanks also go to staff at the Walter Reuther Library for all their patience and help, and special gratitude to Camille Craycraft, whose tireless efforts made this book possible.

INTRODUCTION

Belle Isle ranks as one of the most unique urban parks in the world, and has been a source of great civic pride for Detroiters since the 19th century. An island in the middle of the Detroit River, it is located on the near east side, two miles upriver from the city's center. Measuring nearly two and one half miles in length and one half mile wide, its area covers almost 1,000 acres and consists of nearly limitless facilities. Thousands of city residents have been employed in the development and stewardship of the park's amenities, which include many of Detroit's best-known landmarks, and since the creation of its official park status, millions of people have visited its shores. Because of the island's proximity to the center of Detroit's cultural, habitational, and industrial activity, it has been closely tied to all ranges of civic and economic victory and turmoil. It has been said that, "As Detroit goes, so goes the country," and one may as well reason that "As Belle Isle goes, so goes Detroit"—suggesting that the park has served as a microcosm and demonstration of all of the complex issues of the modern American city.

The 1879 purchase of a large park for the city of Detroit was a controversial, but necessary and natural, event for a place that would later become the greatest industrial center of the world. Already deeply enmeshed in the manufacture of materials that were harvested and mined from the northern part of the state of Michigan, the city's geographical position between the Great Lakes made it a natural hub of trade and commerce. People were pouring into Detroit at an alarming rate in order to work in the factories, and their hard-working lives created a great need for a place of relaxation and recreation away from the factories of the 19th century city.

When the city's people and politicians looked around and saw other great cities of the young nation (especially the Great Lakes cities of Chicago and Milwaukee, which had reserved large flats of water frontage for park use) establishing world-class parks, it was decided that Detroit needed the same. After a long battle between city officials, private interests, and the interests of the citizens, Belle Isle was purchased for $200,000 and the nation's preeminent landscape architect, Frederick Law Olmsted, was hired for its design and development. This book is the photographic history of Detroit's world-class park within the context of Olmsted's vision and the growth of the city it serves.

Called "Wahnabezee" ("Swan Island" or "White Swan") by natives of the region, "Isle aux Cochons" ("Hog Island") by the first French settlers, and renamed "Belle Isle" by Detroiters in the 19th century, the island has grown with the city and has always served as a commons for its citizens. Long appreciated for the natural wonder of its old-growth forest and river vistas, the park has become equipped with modernized facilities in order to absorb Detroit's vast cultural interests and growth in population. Over time, it has also been home to some of the city's greatest tourist attractions and events of national and international concern. But its place as a recreational and nature center for the people of the industrial city has remained its most important asset.

All photographs in this book are from the collections of the Walter P. Reuther Library at Wayne State University, unless otherwise noted. The Reuther Library, located in Detroit, Michigan, houses the Archives of Labor and Urban Affairs. It is home to the United States' largest and most comprehensive collections of original historic materials relating to 20th century labor and urban history. One of the treasures of the Audiovisual Department is the photonegative collection of The Detroit News. The collection, which numbers more than 500,000 images, covers the period from just before 1900 to 1984. The hard work of numerous staff photographers is represented in the collection, including pioneering *News* photographer William Kuenzel. Working with everything from 8 x 10 field cameras to modern 35mm, these staff members left a magnificent visual record for the city of Detroit. The authors of this book are indebted to them for this priceless legacy.

It is therefore the scope of this book to highlight this historic photo collection, and in doing so to limit here the represented timeframe of Belle Isle's history. Although there are over 50 images of Belle Isle, alone, in this collection, few of them date past the 1950s. So then, although the city of Detroit and its wondrous park experienced many transformations and important events in the late 20th century (including a series of yearly Formula One Gran Prix races, new stadiums for its professional sport franchises, a new music industry, and a new corporate world headquarters for its downtown area), those experiences are not covered here.

One

"It Will Rise From the Ashes"
Origins of a Park and its City

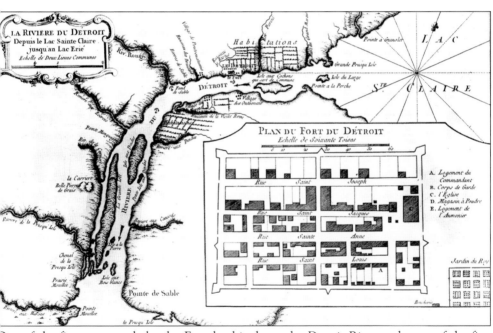

One of the first maps made by the French, this shows the Detroit River and some of the first "habitations" just above Isle aux Cochons, or "Hog Island." The story of the how the island was named is complicated and full of legend. It suggests that when the French first visited the area they found an idol to the Indian God, Manitou, and destroyed it. When natives found the broken idol they gathered the pieces and took them to the island and, magically, the pieces of Manitou turned into rattlesnakes. This might explain why another early name for the place was "Snake Island," and why early settlers released their livestock, including hogs, onto the island to roam freely and reduce the population of snakes. Another native name for the island was Wahnabezee, or Swan Island. (Courtesy of the Burton Historical Collection, Detroit Public Library.)

This etching of the first European settlement of Detroit, Fort Pontchartrain, shows a peaceful though distant, relationship with natives. Teepees front the river next to the French, who traded, hunted, and farmed with native tribes for many years. Just two miles upriver from the location of the old fort, Isle aux Cochons was in these days—as it was until settlement by the English—used as a commons for all the people of the area. (Courtesy of the Burton Historical Collection, Detroit Public Library.)

This is a famous and rather stern-looking portrait of the man who has been considered the "founder" of Detroit for over 300 years, Antoine De Le Mothe Cadillac. Louis XIV commissioned Cadillac to travel down from Montreal through Lake Ontario and Lake Erie to find a place that would serve as a fur trading center for the entire region. When Cadillac found that the narrow straits of the Detroit River and the higher land of the Detroit banks would provide a perfect garrison for protection and an equal distance between the passage north (Lake St. Clair) and passage east, he and his entourage began to make a new settlement. (Courtesy of the Burton Historical Collection, Detroit Public Library.)

10

Born to a Chippewa Mother and an Ottawa Father, Pontiac became the principle chief to many tribes in the Midwest during the mid-18th century. Though he grew up in friendship with French settlers, the arrival of the English and their movement into the territory disturbed him, and eventually led to an important moment in the destiny of Detroit and Belle Isle. During the Pontiac rebellion of 1763, many garrisons and forts in the region fell to tribes following Pontiac's insurgence, until Pontiac himself took on Detroit. Information of the attack had leaked to the English and the rebellion was put down. Upset by this defeat, Pontiac's men went to Hog Island and murdered the three families who were its inhabitants at the time, along with much of the community's livestock. An officer named George McDougall was the only person of the Fischer, Turnbull, and McDougall families to survive, and he would later secure the island's purchase for private use. The defeat of Pontiac at Detroit also safeguarded the rule of the British before the Revolutionary War. (Courtesy of the Burton Historical Collection, Detroit Public Library.)

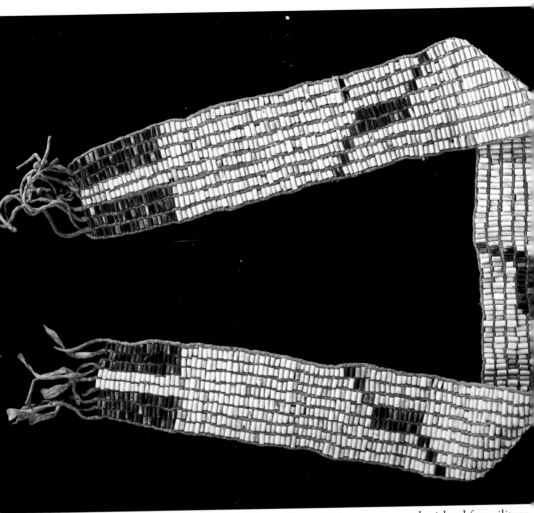

In 1768, King George III gave George McDougall permission to occupy the island for military reasons. McDougall negotiated purchase of the island from the Ottawa and Chippewa for five barrels of rum, three pounds of vermilion, and one belt of wampum, with three barrels of rum and three pounds of paint to be delivered when possession was taken. As was the custom at the time, a twig from the island was given to McDougall as symbolic of possession of the whole. A French settler named DeQuindre had previously tried to gain ownership and once again a long battle ensued when the public discovered McDougall's claim. When the British surrendered American territories after the Revolutionary War, native ownerships were not recognized and heirs to properties once held by the British stood in court. The property was then passed down through the McComb family, and eventually purchased by Barnabus Campau, who would also leave the island to heirs. Shown here is the actual wampum belt used in the McDougall trade. (Courtesy of the Burton Historical Collection, Detroit Public Library.)

Shown here are is the actual deed to Hog Island, authored and signed by Lieutenant George McDougall, and Ojibwa and Ottawa Chiefs Okitchewanong, Couttawyin, and Ottowachkin. The image depicts the pictographic signatures of the Native Chiefs, and comes with an endorsement from the Quebec Register's office of the date received: "January 1777 at one o'clock in the afternoon." The deed was passed from the McDougalls to the McCombs, and finally to the family of Barnabas Campau. Barnabas was the brother of famed Detroiter Joseph, whose father had remarried, after the death of their mother, into none other than the McDougall family. Campau himself would marry his stepmother's granddaughter in his second marriage, and forever tie his lineage solidly to Belle Isle. After Campau died in 1845, he left the island as a legacy to his children. His wife remarried after his death and on the island built a home that still stands today. (Courtesy of the Burton Historical Collection, Detroit Public Library.)

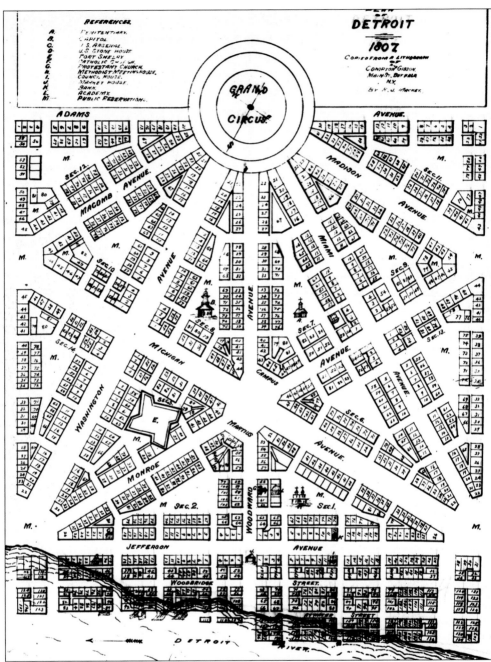

During Campau's life, the city of Detroit was destroyed by fire, burning completely in 1805. Befor
the fire, though, the city had begun to make plans to expand its industry and land area, and t
make room for its growing population. Seen here is the Plan of Detroit, made in 1807 by Augustu
Woodward, a Judge, who would give his own name to the main thoroughfare of this new plan. Th
plan is made from the "spoke" model, like that of Washington, D.C., with streets emanating ou
from a center, and with the river at the foot of Woodward, which served as the hub of trade. Ther
were also plans for schools, banks, a capital (which Detroit became for a time after its statehood
and a penitentiary, but the only park areas were the small squares at road junctions.

14

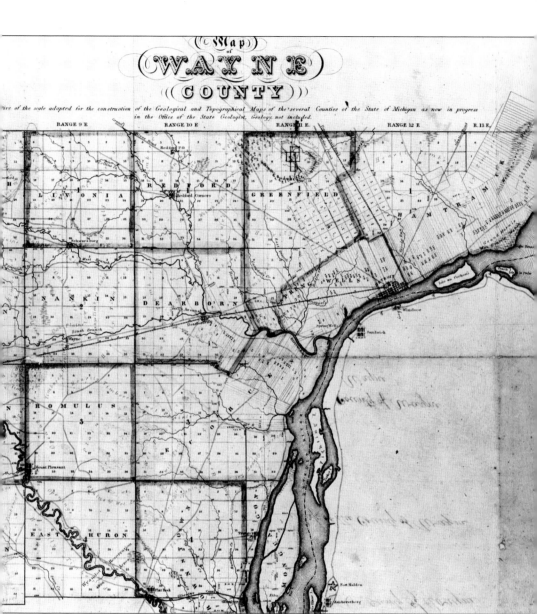

rive of the scale adopted for the construction of the Geological and Topographical Maps of the several Counties of the State of Michigan as now in progress in the Office of the State Geologist, Geology not included.

RANGE 9 E   RANGE 10 E   RANGE 11 E   RANGE 12 E   R. 13 E.

Wayne County was a parceled and divided territory in the mid-19th century, but still primarily populated within the ribbon farms that ran away from the river. More detailed maps of the time show names for every section of ribbon, which tells us how few people inhabited this territory outside of Detroit (the grid at the intersection of Michigan, Grand River, and Gratiot). The areas now known as Hamtramck, Greenfield, and Dearborn are labeled mostly as "Heavily Timbered" by this mapmaker. Springwells (most of which later became Detroit proper), was considered a "suburb" at the time. The city of Detroit's Campus Martius, here within Woodward's plan, was considered the main gathering place of the entire region. Note the strange size depictions of Windsor and Sandwich, across the river in Canada; this informs us of how closely Detroit and Windsor grew up together.

The Detroit industries of iron smelting and lumber processing and shipping experienced a boom in the mid-19th century, fueled by the opening of the Erie Canal and the flow of labor from the East to the West. This image gives a good impression of the growth of the city's industry and its river traffic. The Michigan Central Railroad roundhouse is pictured at lower left; Woodward Avenue runs through the middle of town and down to the river, at center. Still, one did not have to travel far from the city to be in vastly unpopulated territory.

Built in 1880 to better deal with the overwhelming amount of market activity downtown, the Central Market Building in Cadillac Square at Campus Martius sits in front of the old, outdoor market structure. The roof of the outdoor market was eventually taken to Belle Isle and used for the horse barn, located on the far east side of the island. At the top of the photo, in a ghostly smudge on the horizon, is Belle Isle, which had just recently been purchased by the city at the time of this photo.

Residing a short distance from the entrance of Belle Isle was the Michigan Stove Company, which later merged with Detroit Stove Works and became the Michigan Stove Works. Using products mined in the Upper Peninsula, then shipped to Detroit for firing and casting, these stove companies were the most successful and prosperous in the world. This is an image of the enormous replica of the company's well-known symbol, the Garland, which was built for the Columbian Exhibition of 1893 and for many years sat near the entrance of the Belle Isle Bridge on Jefferson Avenue.

After the fur trade, a great second wave of industry hit the region, this time consisting of lumber, ore, and copper. Especially after the opening of the Sault Ste. Marie locks, which made shipping from the Upper Peninsula much easier, raw materials flowed down to be reconstituted for steel and a new, Midwestern Iron Age was born. With the influx of such industry, it is easy to see why Detroit became the leading maker of Pullman cars, ships, and later automobiles, but also easy to see why the people of the city wanted a large public park for recreation.

Belle Isle is the shadow in the top of the photograph, which was taken around the time the city decided it needed a large-scale park and made the purchase in 1879. Dominating the image is the Michigan Central Railroad and its "roundhouse," used to rotate train engines onto different tracks. Ships would come down from Lake Huron and Lake St. Clair, or up from Lakes Erie and Ontario to deliver or pick up materials from these trains. Before Belle Isle was purchased for use as a park, many wealthy businessmen and politicians wanted to make the island into an industrial center—and some wanted to use it as a switching yard like this one to better perform trade with Canada, if a tunnel or bridge could also be financed.

Parke, Davis & Co., Home Office and Laboratories. Detroit, Mich. U. S. (

This image reveals much about the city's industrial and recreational past. The manufacturing building here is the home of Park, Davis & Co., which by 1891 had become one of the world's leading makers of pharmaceuticals. In the lower right corner of the photo is the original home of the Detroit Boat Club. Founded in 1839, the DBC is the oldest club of its kind in the United States. It began to run operations from this location in 1872. Located at the foot of Joseph Campau Avenue, below Jefferson, the Boat Club remained there until it opened its first clubhouse on Belle Isle in 1891.

Now called "the Whitehouse," this building actually predates Belle Isle's park status, and is the only building left on the island that predates the city's purchase. After the death of Barnabas Campau, his wife, Archange (granddaughter of Cpt. George McDougall), remarried to R. Storrs Willis and built this house on the Canadian shore in 1863. They called it Insulruhe, the name of the street on which it still stands. The building was renovated in 1984 by the Friends of Belle Isle, and now houses the official offices of the park.

Opened in 1882, this building also predates the park in many respects. It marked what was then the east and southernmost point on the island and served as light source for traffic coming down from Lake St. Clair. With the addition of further territory onto the island in the early 20th century, it was razed, and a Coast Guard Station is located there today. It was called St. Clair Lifeboat Station until St. Clair Shores erected its own, when it was renamed Station Belle Isle. The light at the top of this structure is still in use at Livingstone, Belle Isle's current lighthouse. (Courtesy of the Detroit Historical Museums.)

This is an image of the intersection of Jefferson and Rivard, in what is now considered Grosse Pointe, just upriver from Belle Isle. The photo depicts what many streets looked like around the time of the purchase of the island—unpaved and dirty, and obviously not prepared for what was to come in the world of transportation in the next half century. At the time, Grosse Pointe was still largely a haven of retreat, almost a vacation spot, for the more affluent classes of Detroit. Jefferson Ave is the main thoroughfare that runs closest to the water and follows the river for miles of urban and suburban territory.

Around the time that Belle Isle was purchased, the Office of the Mayor in the city of Detroit was a revolving door, mayor-council type of government. George C. Langdon was the Mayor when the city bought Belle Isle, and the purchase was his only standout effort. Partly because on the island was planned a water intake for the city (and thus making Belle Isle more than "just" a park), plans were moving ahead when Langdon took office. The succeeding Mayor, William G. Thompson, took more liberal steps toward giving Board of Park Commissions power over spending, but these efforts mostly failed. The park struggled in its early days to secure funds for improvements during his term. Pictured here is Detroit's second City Hall, when the population was approximately 100,000. Dignitaries and city businessmen often had as much as or more influence in government affairs than the city's highest-ranking official.

The battle to get a large park for the city was a monumental struggle for its proponents, partly due to cost, partly due to location (some wanted to annex a part of Hamtramck, which at the time ran all the way to the river), and partly due to private interest. When the city decided on the purchase of the island for $200,000, it issued Park Fund Bonds to help pay for the land and initial improvements. The problem with using bonds to fund a facility such as a park is that revenue from funds is not a stable, ongoing source, because it is not a permanent appropriation of the city's budget. Frederick Law Olmsted, the famed landscape architect contracted to design Bell Isle, quickly identified a problem with this kind of funding and pleaded with city officials to establish a more stable method of support. (Courtesy of the Detroit Historical Museums.)

Park Commissioners pictured here, from left to right, are Benjamin Hoyt, William Guni Ed Van Lyon, William Maybury, P.H.A. Barkley, and Halbert in 1898. Created by the Pa Act of 1871 the Board of Park Commissioners often had a broad focus in its first years. first job was to investigate where a park would best be purchased and at what cost. Al under their consideration was the creation of the Grand Boulevard, itself a kind of par a place for a water intake sufficient for the expanding city, and for a tunnel and bridge Canada. When Belle Isle was first purchased, all of these considerations were focused on tl island itself. (Courtesy of the Detroit Historical Museums.)

22

ictured here is Cass Park in the late 19th century. As late as 1844, most sites of present-day
arks in Detroit were ponds and marshlands, and "used as a place of deposit for refuse of every
ind" (Farmer). By 1883, Detroit had built 17 parks, beginning with the construction of Grand
ircus Park (just north of the city's center) in 1846. Most parks were small, half-acre plats of green
esigned to break up neighborhoods and give the appearance of a more cultivated environment.
ass Park was just such a place—located in a neighborhood just northwest of the city center, it
oasted a fountain and a block's worth of greenage to calm and soothe the city dweller.

ith industry and the population that supported it rapidly expanding, residents and the
ltural elite wanted a truly recreational park that would suit the image they sought to
oject. Since the inhabitants of Detroit, like most other new cities at the time, were
iropeans (or descendants of Europeans), their models in city planning were reminiscent of
irope's. Central Park (pictured above), which itself was modeled after Parisian causeways
id parks, would provide the template, and the city hired its designer, Frederick Law
lmsted, to shape Belle Isle into a place of world-class stature. (Courtesy of the National
irk Service, Frederick Law Olmsted National Historic Site.)

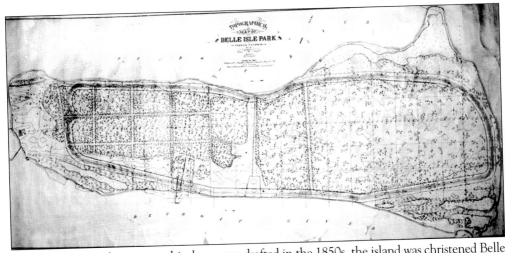

At about the time this topographical map was drafted in the 1850s, the island was christened Belle Isle, but the idea of transforming it into a park for the city was still a fantasy. Since the island rose only a foot above the river in many places, it was very marshy territory. On the lower left and right (lower east and west) we can see the beginnings of Lake Takoma and Okonoka. Olmsted's idea was to fill in these marshy territories, partly because they were thought to breed mosquitoes, and the people of the city were worried about disease carried by the bugs. Nobody would want to visit an island where one could catch scarlet fever. Filling in the marshes could be done simply by excavating land from higher territories and depositing it in the lowlands, and thereby creating greater pasture. Also prominent on this map is a ferry dock at the head of the island, which by the 1850s was already being used by the ferry companies to deliver passengers for recreational purposes. (Courtesy of the Detroit Historical Museums.)

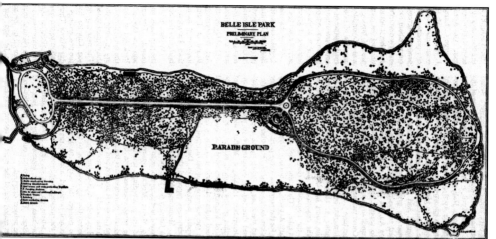

BELLE ISLE PARK
PRELIMINARY PLAN

PARADE GROUND

lmsted's plan was a simple one, and he wanted to keep it that way because he was aware of the rangling, infighting, and penny-pinching that occurred amongst city officials. His plan was develop only the far western part of the island and build just a refectory, marching ground, oathouses, and police stations—all close to the ferry dock. The ferry dock itself would be the land's most prominent feature, with a connecting shelter to span the entire length of the land's west end. This part of his plan was quickly rejected (though a six-hundred-foot shelter as built), but his idea of creating a system of canals to drain the island's swampy, low-lying nd was used. Olmsted was insistent upon "the genius of the place"—that the island's natural auty and untouched vistas would provide more profound pleasure than any structure man uld build. He suggested just one main road, Central Avenue, which would extend down its nter to get wanderers and riders through to the opposite end.

pposite: Frederick Law Olmsted was the premier landscape architect of the 19th century, d though his plans for Belle Isle were carried through only in part, his ideas for the park's anagement and his insistence on planning for the park's future can be felt today. Traveling road at an early age, he was exposed to the ways in which the old, metropolitan European ies retained natural vistas; this gave him an awareness of the possibilities for the new urban rain that was developing in a young America. In his early days he partnered with Calvert aux and was commissioned to develop Central Park in New York. Afterward, he worked on his vn to design park systems for many of the nation's great cities, including Washington, Boston, nicago, Milwaukee, and Buffalo. (Photo courtesy of the National Park Service, Frederick Law lmsted National Historic Site.)

PARK FOR DETROIT:

BEING

A PRELIMINARY CONSIDERATION OF CERTAIN PRIME
CONDITIONS OF ECONOMY FOR THE

BELLE ISLE SCHEME,

DESIGNED TO FURTHER DETERMINATIVE DISCUSSION OF THE
LASTING INTERESTS OF THE CITY IN THE MATTER,
WITH A VIEW TO

A SETTLED POLICY;

WITH

A SUGGESTION OF THE DISTINCTIVE CHARACTER OF A
PARK ADAPTED TO THE LOCAL CIRCUMSTANCES,
AND AN OUTLINE OF THE LEADING
FEATURES OF A SUITABLE

PERMANENT PLAN OF OPERATIONS.

" With this intent in view, I may, I think, hope to move you, I do not say to
agree with all I urge upon you, yet, at least, to think the matter worth thinking
about." — WILLIAM MORRIS.

RICHMOND, BACKUS & CO.,
PUBLISHERS
DETROIT,

Though Olmsted had already been on the job for two years, this "plan" was more of a plea than a blueprint. The architect himself paid for multiple copies of the 62-page document to be distributed to various Detroit dignitaries. He hoped to win their political and financial support, though he rightly perceived a growing distrust of his ideas. New York's Central Park proved to be an expensive project and city officials were wary of Olmsted running up the tab on Belle Isle. But the plan insisted upon simplicity, and even warned that the construction of "churches, theaters, dance-houses, race courses, museums, collections in zoology, botany, mineralogy, and horticultural exhibitions . . . can be better placed elsewhere than on Belle Isle." He estimated that his plan would cost a million dollars and would produce "through the silent persuasion of nature . . . [a place that] for centuries be growing, year after year, richer sylvan picturesqueness and sylvan stateliness." Olmsted soon left the project when he became convinced that city officials were going to do whatever they wanted, with or without his plan and advice. Asked later about his stewardship of the park he said, "I know nothing of the place." (Courtesy of the Detroit Historical Museums.)

26

Two

"Genius of the Place"

entral Avenue, the straight walking and riding promenade through the middle of the island, pictured here, c. 1900. The simplicity of this tree-lined avenue is perfectly consistent with msted's plans for other major cities—a place for men and women of all classes to congregate d spend their leisure time together. The opening of the park in 1882 was also a revisitation to e past, because even though many people used Belle Isle as a place of recreation in the 19th ntury, it was privately owned and its purchase by the city was a return to the days when the tive people of the region used the island as a commons.

Pictured here is the ferry dock and first bathhouse in its original location, *c.* 1900. A fraction of the size of the one Olmsted's plans called for, this ferry dock would serve millions of people over the 50 years it was in operation. Note the flagpole at left—it was transplanted from Recreation Park, home of the Detroit's first professional baseball team, and the National League Pennant was raised upon it in 1887.

This flyer, from the park's first year of "official" operation, is an ad from the Detroit, Belle Isle & Windsor Ferry Co. Ferries delivered pleasure-seekers to the island for years prior to its purchase by the city and opening as a park. There's even a poem here that alludes to the island's former names. Many different tales describe how the park got its current moniker. The most believable suggests that picnickers from the Detroit Boat Club decided that Hog Island was not eloquent enough for a place of such beauty. These folks apparently gave it the name "Belle" (beauty), possibly after Isabelle Cass, daughter of then-Governor Lewis Cass. (Courtesy of the Detroit Historical Museums.)

hese drawings
epict the steamer,
ortune, loaded
ith Belle Isle-
ound passengers,
nd advertises
pening day of
e season: May
2, 1894. The first
dvertisement
in German,
hose population
nd influence in
etroit at the turn
the century was
normous. Because
the abundance
work in the
ty's industries,
etroit was a place
great destiny for
migrants from
e East coast,
d Germans
mmanded the greatest ethnic majority. (Courtesy of
ossin Great Lakes Museum.)

BELLE ISLE PARK.

Eröffnung der Saison '94.

Vr. Samstag, den 12. Mai 1894, an, werden
regelmäßig täglich von 9.30 Uhr ab alle dreißig
Minuten Dampfer vom Fuß der Woodward Ave.
und der Jos. Campau Ave. nach dem Inselpark
abfahren.   10m13t

BELLE ISLE PARK
1894 OPENING!

Regular Steamers from Woodward and
Campau Aves.

Detroit, Belle Isle and Windsor Ferry Co., Owners.

BELLE ISLE PASSENGER FERRY, EXCURSION AND WRECKING STEAMER, "PROMISE."

Length, 132 feet.	Draught, 12 feet.	Capacity, 2,500 passengers.
Beam,, water line, 31½ feet.	Speed, 15 miles per hour.	Allowed by Government, 1,200.
" top sides, 39½ feet.	Two Scotch boilers, 10 feet shell, 12½ feet long.	Cost, $50,000.
" on deck, 51 feet.	Engines triple, 22 x 22 x 22 x 24 inches.	Built by the Detroit Dry Dock Company.

WALTER E. CAMPBELL, Pres't.   HORACE W. AVERY, Sec'y.

nother ad from the Detroit, Belle Isle, and Windsor Ferry Co., this one advertises the steamer
omise, and contains the ship's specifications. Of particular note is the ship's capacity, listed at
500 passengers, followed by the caveat that the government will allow less than half of that.
Courtesy of the Detroit Historical Museums.)

This "live action" photograph of the *Promise* from the turn of the century may expose the ferry company's violation of government allowances for capacity. Though the first bridge to Belle Isle was constructed and opened in 1889, catching the ferry downtown proved much easier for many. And, of course, there was the extra entertainment of riding a great steamer.

This painting from 1895 shows the constructed island with all of its "modern" facilities. From the beginning, the park was a destination for all seasons, but during winter months the park had shorter hours because of the extended time the swing bridge remained impassable and open for river traffic. (Courtesy of the Detroit Historical Museums.)

he point where Woodward Ave intersected the Detroit River was the principal place to catch
he ferries c. 1910s. These were the ships of the Detroit, Belle Isle, and Windsor Ferry Co.,
rger boats than those that carried passengers across the shorter route via the foot of the Belle
e Bridge. The 2-mile ride up the river to Belle Isle cost 10¢ from this location, but one could
so cross to Windsor, Ontario for 5¢.

Because the island rose only a foot above the Detroit River, a scheme was needed to drain i swampy terrain. Part of Olmsted's plan was to dig canals along the straight avenue that head out to the forested area of the West end, and looped back around the woods. The city's revis plan was to dig more canals, but also to make lakes of the marshlands on the western a eastern ends of the island and to use the canals to connect the lakes. (Courtesy of the Detr Historical Museums.)

This is another photograph of the construction of the canal system, much of which was do by hand. Thousands of men worked digging canals, reclaiming marshland, and making roa over a period of about 15 years. The project cost far more to create and maintain, and to much longer than Olmsted's original estimates, but the new plans helped to create a park w greater all-season use.

This photograph, c. 1888, shows workers digging the marshy area that would become Lake Muskoday. Again, excavating by hand required the effort of thousands of men who were grateful for the employment in the economic depression of the 1890s. Three lakes were created during these years: Takoma, Okonoka, and Muskoday. (Courtesy of the Detroit Historical Museums.)

Reclaiming the marshland also meant that the earth extracted could be used elsewhere. The digging of Lake Muskoday provided the fill necessary to build another perimeter roadway, Riverbank Road, which ran through the northern and easternmost point of the island, now inhabited by the Detroit Yacht Club.

Thinning the undergrowth and clearing some of the forestation was one way in which Olmste believed the park could help pay for itself—at least in the beginning. Though these photograph are from the winter of 1931, they reveal the important sawmill industry that operated on the islan for many years, in the area now inhabited by the offices and maintenance of the park.

Not only would the thinning of trees on the island provide for a more passable and invitir landscape, it would provide raw materials for the construction of the island's infrastructure—i bridges and buildings. What wasn't needed for construction on the island could be sold a market value and subtracted from the park's cost.

This next series of photographs shows the process of harvesting ice, another small industry believed to help the park sustain itself. Ice was harvested in winter and stored in a large facility that provided refrigerated beverages for the island's many visitors through the warmer months. This photograph shows the horse-plowed cutting of ice into manageable cubes on the island's lakes, this one most likely Lake Tacoma.

This photograph, taken c. 1936, shows the second step in harvesting ice—sending it through the canal system to a storage facility.

Finally, the ice was sent up conveyors into an icehouse and stacked high for the benefit of par visitors in the summer months.

Olmsted's plan was to build one enormous main shelter pavilion connected to the ferry dock which would run the length of the island at its western end in order to create a central meetir place and main comfort station. Called a "shed" of "colossal folly" by critical newspapers of th day, this plan was abandoned in favor of many smaller facilities throughout the island. Th pavilion pictured here was one of the original shelters, located near the ferry docks. Many the original shelters remain today.

The Detroit Yacht Club formed in 1868, and was incorporated in 1887. Its first clubhouse on Belle Isle was purchased from the Michigan Yacht Club when the MYC became financially insolvent. That first structure burned in 1904; a second building, pictured, was built and the DYC moved in the next year. This building cost $20,540 and served members until a larger clubhouse of greater facility was built in 1923.

The old Casino was completed the same year as Tacoma Lake and the first Canoe Shelter, in 1887. later burned and was razed in 1908. Somewhat an alternative to Olmsted's enormous ferry dock avilion, the idea of the Casino was to create a place that could house elegant events and serve rst-class meals to park visitors. Designed in the Victorian style, it spanned 8,000 square feet. Courtesy of the Burton Historical Collection, Detroit Public Library.)

Called the Boat House or the Canoe Shelter, this facility rented small craft boats to park attendees for many years. Located near the Casino on Lake Tacoma, the building was a short walk from the ferry dock. From here canoeists could travel east to the other lakes and through the forests at the other end of the island. At the height of canoe use on the island, in the 1920s, rentals exceeded 40,000 per year. This photo was taken c.1900. (Courtesy of the Detroit Historical Museums.)

In 1882, Park Commissioners enlisted the Detroit Opera House Orchestra to give weekly concerts on the island, at the band shell that was perched over a canal close to the entrance to the park. The events could be enjoyed from permanent seating installed on the banks of the canal, or on the canal itself, while floating in a canoe. This photograph, c. 1910s, reveals the popularity of the orchestra concerts, witnessed from both land and water.

Taken c. 1931, this aerial photograph shows the main bridge approach (at top) and gives a good ide of what island patrons saw when they entered the park. The Casino is out of the photograph, lowe left, the ferry dock is also out of the photograph, upper left. Central in the picture is the gazeb band shelter with permanent seating on either side of the canal banks, up and downstream.

Another photograph of the bridge approach in the early days, this one taken in May of 1904, shows the old bridge approach at left, and one of the island's first stone canal bridges in the center. In total there are 21 smaller bridges on the island, most of which were first made of wood, reconstructed with iron, and then concrete.

Opened a year after the park's unveiling, Central Avenue Bridge was made of wood and stone. This photograph dates to c. 1900, and reveals the kind of traffic typical of the island in those days—horse and buggy and pedestrian.

Not at all the Keystone Cops, police on the island have always had much work to do. Thi photograph shows the first Police Station and the city's finest in 1889. Even as Olmsted drew up his plans in 1882, he was wary of the potential for vandalism and roguishness if the park was no properly made. There was malicious damage to the park before its official opening, and Olmsted plans suggested that the city be careful to make Belle Isle a place that inspires a love for one environs, writing: "one of the most important elements of value in a park, never to be lost sight c in a study of its economics, is its power to divert men from unwholesome, vicious, and destructive methods and habits of seeking recreation." It is the "poor park that does not, through the impression of its fitness . . . inspire enough respect to serve as a check upon the propensities thus evinced . . . Olmsted's idea, in other words, is that a great park inspires people to act well by the virtue of the atmosphere. Police in a perfect park, then, would almost be unnecessary.

This is the new police station, c. 1894. Its peaked tile roofs and fieldstone exterior are distinctive and representative of the other Victorian buildings on the island at the time. In 1927 it was the first to broadcast dispatches to police cars—the middle room, upstairs at center, served as the control room. Completed in 1893, the building is evidence of its own architectural integrity, as it continues to serve as the island's Police Station today.

This photo shows the island's main barn and shops, completed in 1894. A mixture of Tudor and Victorian architecture, this enormous facility served as the park maintenance center, and still does so today.

This is the Detroit Boat Club's second clubhouse as it appeared c. 1898. The first was opened 1891, and then burned in 1893. This facility opened in 1894 and burned in 1901. Realizing pattern (one that would plague many of the island's early structures), Alpheus Chittenden v commissioned to build a fireproof, concrete structure. The issue of building private clubs with a park designated for public use has long been a topic of debate, especially since long-term lea for properties were handed out for $1 per year.

n 1902, this new Boat Club was opened, the third in just over 10 years. This one was built to ast—made of concrete and designed by Chittenden in Spanish Renaissance style. This picture is n early shot of the river-side exterior, before docks were constructed. At lower right, under the pen-air veranda, is the storage space for the clubs' sculling boats and pleasure canoes.

his shot shows the island-side entrance, and was taken after the club had matured and ndscaping had been done. The club featured an Olympic-sized pool, where many swim meets ok place over the years, including the qualifying meet for Johnny Weismuller, who would win gold medal in the 1928 Olympics and later become best known for playing Tarzan in the films. he sign on the entrance walk says: "Detroit Boat Club—Private."

Located between the ferry dock and the bridge, the old Bath House was completed in 1894. Thi
photograph was taken c. 1901 and the Bath House burned not long after. A new facility and
bathing beach were situated further east on the island, this time on the other side of the bridge.

Where Olmsted imagined a parade ground (perhaps not anticipating the overwhelming
popularity of baseball to come), the Athletic Pavilion was built. Built in 1905 and still in
use today, the building's architecture is reminiscent of the peaked roofs and cupolas of other
Victorian buildings of the island. There are baseball and softball diamonds on the grounds
serving thousands of players and leagues around the city, as well as tennis courts, an Olympic
size track, and space enough for any number of other athletic activities.

Initial work to build a zoo on the island began in 1886 when a deer park was established. Olmsted warned against such facilities because of their cost, but the city kept building attractions such as this Bear Den (pictured) and a Wolf Cage in the 1890s. First founded at the corner of Michigan and Trumbull (later famous for baseball in the city), the Detroit Zoo would eventually move to Belle Isle in 1909, and then to the suburb of Royal Oak in 1956, just after Detroit started downsizing the island's facilities. Made into a Children's Zoo after the Royal Oak move, it then became a "Safari, Land Zoo" in 1980. In 2001, what remained of the island's zoo was "temporarily" closed because of city budgets.

This image depicts an unusually unpopulated moment at the Skating Pavilion in 1919. Skating on the lakes and canals of the island in the early-to-mid-20th century was as popular as canoeing in the warm weather months. Again we see the grand Victorian architecture that resembles the other early structures of the park, though this one is capped with a panoramic "bird's nest" for views across the island. (Courtesy of the Detroit Historical Museums.)

Near the Casino and the Skating Pavilion was the Cedar Mount. Created from the soil dug to make the canals in the area, the Cedar Mount was a landmark for many years. At the top was a grotto, on one side was a fountain, and on the other a horticultural message board. In its early days, this manicured mound of dirt led to the firing of one park official when he was charged with over-landscaping and making the area too fanciful.

ICE WATER DRINKING FOUNTAINS, BELLE ISLE PARK.

This page from *A Souvenir of Belle Isle* shows some of the many different drinking fountains that were installed for the park's opening. The most famous of these is the one in the middle, the Newsboy Fountain, which remains on the island as a statue. This was the first memorial on the island, brought there by James E. Scripps, founder of the *Detroit News*. The newsboy has been stolen many times over the years, but either returned or replaced every time.

Opened in 1904 (when these photographs were taken), the Belle Isle Aquarium is the oldest public facility of its kind in the United States. Albert Kahn (then with Nettleton & Kahn) also had his hand in the designing this structure. The exterior features a copper roof and elaborate stone work at its joined walls and cornices.

The interior of the Aquarium is covered in green tile made by Pewabic Pottery and equipped with 44 wall tanks and three floor pools. The highlight of daily events is still the feeding of the electric eels, which glow brightly when being fed. At its peak in attendance, around 1940, the Aquarium hosted upwards of two million visitors per year.

50

Also opened in 1904, and standing beside the Aquarium, is the Belle Isle Horticulture Building (Conservatory). Its domed greenhouses of glass were originally framed in wood until a complete reconstruction in the 1950s replaced the frame with steel. The site of large shows for spring tulips, fall mums, and summer dahlias, the Conservatory houses facilities for a fernery display, an orchid room, a palm house, a cactus exhibit, and a tropical plants section. The surrounding three acres are also cultivated for formal gardens, and contain 20 greenhouses. In 1955 the structure was rededicated and renamed the Anna Scripps Whitcomb Conservatory.

Opened in 1908 and also designed by Detroit's preeminent architect, Albert Kahn—designer of some of the world's larger manufacturing facilities—the contemporary Casino was what was perceived to be necessary for a city of such growing stature. A few of its prominent features are vaulted ceiling and marble floors in the ballroom, and a second-story veranda that surveys the entire west end of the park. A number of different restaurants have operated from within the structure throughout the 20th century, usually privately controlled but sometimes run by the city. The height of first-class food service was in the 1920s, when approximately 10,000 dinners were served. When opened it was said to be "the most complete and finest casino in the United States."

With the new Bath House, which held 800 dressing rooms, the facility could accommodate 000 bathers at a time. In 1916, a room, towel, and rental of a bathing suit cost 10¢; a suit 'ithout a locker cost 5¢.

'hen built, the Bath House was one of the largest facilities of its kind in the world. When the w Bath House and bathing beach opened in 1909, the same year that construction began the new Highland Park Ford plant, the city laid the nation's first concrete pavement (on 'oodward between Six and Seven Mile Roads), and the Tigers won the American League nnant for the third year in a row.

A long-view shot of the first bridge and the activity around the old bridge approach. To th right, above the bridge was Electric Park, an amusement park. One can get a good idea of th experience of attending the amusement park, situated next to the Detroit Stove Works, k knowing the park's attractions through reading the signs (left to right): "Electric Park Pi Pavilion," "Midget City," "Auto Ride," and "Tea Garden." Eventually, the amusement par took up both sides of the bridge approach, adding a roller coaster and other attractions. Th sign above the entrance to the bridge simply reads: "Belle Isle Bridge." There is a fishing pi just to the left of the bridge entrance, and one can see the ferry dock and first bathhouse at th head of the island, at top center.

Opened in 1889, the steel "swing" bridge used wooden planking for its road surface. When a truck carrying construction materials accidentally dropped hot coals while crossing the bridge, the wooden planks began to burn uncontrollably, and the bridge fell into the river. Before the fire, city planners were considering improvements to the island, including a wider bridge that would better accommodate the automobile, bus, trolley, and pedestrian traffic.

In a spectacular moment (postcards were even printed of the event), an arsenal of city firemen attempted to douse the blaze from the bridge's surface, as well as from boats in the river, but it burned beyond repair on April 27, 1915.

At the time of the fire on the first bridge, the busiest intersection in the city was Jefferson and East Grand Boulevard—in part because of the industry of the area, and in part because of the popularity of Belle Isle and Electric Park (at right). The growth of the city and the rapid popularity of the automobile can be understood simply by noting a few details in this photo. The streets are made of brick (and under construction), and there are trolley tracks running horizontally, along Jefferson. There is also bicycle and pedestrian traffic that must contend with the cars and busses (station middle left, next to Belle Isle Park Waiting Room, on East Grand) but there are no traffic lights. Tacked to trees and utility poles (center) are tiny street signs that could not possibly be read unless in very close proximity, and traveling at a slow pace. The next century would see great changes in the way Detroiters processed the details of their city, and their view of the nation and world beyond.

Three

ISLAND IN THE CITY'S AGE OF EXPERIENCE
1900s TO 1960s

Looking from the western edge of the island toward the skyline of downtown Detroit at sunset, one cannot help but reflect upon the past of the city and its park, as well to ponder their future. This view, from August of 1958, looks across the river to the manufacturing sites on the waterfront which shaped Detroit's history and character, while also visible is the downtown area that sprung up from the city's industrial success. As the city's main place of congregation in the 20th century, Belle Isle would serve almost as a mirror to the social highs and lows of Detroit.

Maps on this page and the next, from 1905 and 1912, demonstrate the industrial and residentia development of the city over a seven-year period—from the time of the birth of the automobil until its rapid intensification in manufacturing. By 1906, the Detroit River was the world busiest inland water channel, and much of the city clings to its waterfront. Highland Park where Henry Ford would build his first mass production facility of magnitude, is still a fa distant destination from the downtown center.

uring the first 20 years of the 20th century, the city's population more than tripled, from just
ver a quarter million in 1900 to nearly a million in 1920. By 1914, Ford Motor Company
ffered the $5 workday and the city absorbed people seeking employment and fair wages from all
ver the world. At the time this map was made, the Highland Park plant was nearly completed
d Ford's next area of development, in Dearborn, was still largely farmland. Naturally, the
ardworking people of the city needed a place to recreate, and the number of visitors to Belle
le began to skyrocket.

This image of Campus Martius (the city center, named for Mars, the God of war), looking north shows Detroit just after the birth of the automobile. Trolleys shared the streets with carriages and automobiles, and at night were lit by the tall light towers (center) that often crackled and showered sparks. At the turn of the 20th century, advances in construction and profits in the city's industry were pushing buildings upward, which just before the turn of the century rarely rose above four or five stories.

Representing mass transportation at the turn of the century, this is a typical phaeton—a carriage built Detroiters had multiple choices of ways to get to Belle Isle, including trolley and streetcar, horse and buggy, phaeton, and ferry, at the turn of the century. The automobile was added to this list, at first available to the city's more privileged classes, but soon affordable enough for the masses.

ictured here is a room in the first Oldsmobile plant, also the first "mass production" facility for
ne automobile. Before it burned and Oldsmobile moved to Lansing, this plant was located on
fferson Avenue, very close to the entrance of Belle Isle, as were many of Detroit's important
anufacturing facilities. In 1904, Detroit made 20,000 cars, but in 1917 it made one million.

1891, Mayor Pingree broke ground for the construction of Grand Boulevard (pictured here).
riginally, the boulevard was intended as a parkway for riding and biking, and was positioned as a
rder around the city. Though the city quickly extended past the boundaries of the boulevard, the
ute has always ended on the east side, at the foot of Belle Isle, like a parkway straight to the city's
eat park. In the early days, boulevards were the responsibility of the city's Park Commissioner.

The sign over the vehicles (at left) in this 1909 photograph says "Auto Station." Located just over the bridge and near the Ferry Dock, one could pay 20¢ for a tour of the 700-acre island with stops at the Casino and the Aquarium. One could tour by phaeton or autobus. To simply ride across the bridge, to Jefferson and East Grand Boulevard, required a 3¢ fare.

This is the mass production facility that would change everything—the Highland Park Ford Plant. The advent of the moving production line, which made the manufacture of automobiles much faster and less expensive, was implemented in this plant. From Highland Park would come Ford's first great claim to fame, the Model T, and with it a completely new pace and way of life for the 20th century. Along with it would come the next great wave of migration to the city of Detroit.

he Bus Station at Belle Isle and its drivers and workers are pictured here, c. late 1910s. There
ere several different types and sizes of gasoline-powered buses that ran routes to the island,
en in the early days of bus service. There were those that looked like tractor-trailers, and the
ises pictured here, which were not too much larger than an average step van.

he site of the bus station was chosen for its central location—close to the bathing beaches and
sinos. Built in the early 1900s, it features two open areas where passengers can wait in comfort
incoming and departing vehicles, convenient considering the nature of gas-powered mass transit
at was to come. Eventually, the Motor City abandoned its rail lines in favor of bus routes.

Short-lived, this filling station operated in the 1920s. Even though park usage figur were in the millions during this time, and many accessed the island by car, the gas stati eventually closed down.

Electric Park (also known by the name Riverside Park, among others) was in operation betwe 1906 and 1927. Located on both sides of the Belle Isle Bridge and just below Jefferson Aven it was considered the Coney Island of Detroit. Since Belle Isle was Detroit's premier destinati for recreation seekers, the amusement park was a stop along the way to the island. Through t years, some of Electric Park's largest venues were destroyed by fire, and finally in 1927, it w condemned and razed to make way for a more traditional grassy park.

Newsboy Day at Electric Park was a busy event every year. Both Belle Isle and Electric Park played host to the paperboys, whose day out was sponsored by the *Detroit News*. After a time on the rides at the amusement park or dancing at the huge ballrooms that were famous at the time, the newsboys would hop a ferry to the island.

When the first Belle Isle Bridge burned in 1915, a new, temporary bridge was quickly built. At the time the bridge burned, part of Electric Park was demolished to make way for the temporary bridge approach. In addition to the array of automobile models, the old signs for the factories of the Detroit Stove Works—world leader in stove manufacturing—are visible to the left of the bridge at top.

Seen here is another view of the temporary bridge, this time from the air—a perspective no possible ten years before the bridge fire. Also visible is the new bridge, well under construction At bottom right is the Detroit Boat Club. Dominating this c. late 1910s photo is a seaplane another sight unseen in the previous decade.

isure seekers wait in line by the hundreds to board the ferry to Belle. The massive industrial owth of the city brought in millions of people in a very short time, thus placing the burden free recreation on the city's premier park. Note that the majority of men are wearing straw its in this c. late 1910s photo. The Boat Club is visible at center, top.

lso from the late 1910s, this is another photo of ferry riders, this time on the island side. The owd is obviously conscious of the photographer as they exit ferries or wait to be transported ck to the city. This may, as well, be Newsboy Day, or a similar day of special events often heduled throughout the warm weather months.

Cedar Mount, made from dredgings of the canals, is captured in this c. 1916 photo, just befor the United States entered into the First World War. The Veterans of Foreign Wars floral desig was made to memorialize, especially, those who served in the Spanish American War, als commemorated by another permanent memorial on the park's Central Avenue.

This next series of photographs documents the important position of Belle Isle during the tim of Prohibition. Located on the river between Windsor and Detroit, Belle Isle was geographicall and literally right in the middle of the issue. In 1918, Michigan adopted Prohibition, whic continued for the better part of 15 years, though alcohol poured in from Canada for th duration. Winter was an especially productive time for rumrunners, who would risk drivin across the frozen river to pick up booze, often pulling skiffs or rowboats for extra cargo.

his is the truck of a rumrunner that fell through the ice on Lake St. Clair in 1926. Ontario, anada prohibited the sale of liquor for a time as well, but not its manufacturing. Before the ɔening of the Ambassador Bridge and Windsor Tunnel, the best way to get liquor made in anada was simply to take a boat across the two-mile channel, or to drive in winter. From ɔledo, Ohio to Port Huron, about 75 percent of liquor smuggled into the U.S. during ɔhibition came across the Michigan-Ontario waterway.

There were many boat slips along the Canadian shore, and while rumrunners had to worry about their cargo when crossing back to Detroit, they also worried about being robbed for their liquor money on the trip over. Here, a boat has pulled up to a waiting freight car whose contents were unloaded into the boat's hull. Because Belle Isle was halfway across the river, rumrunners had to travel half the distance to safely deliver their goods to waiting buyers.

Opposite, Top: Because organized crime lords had such enormous financial resources, they could afford to buy the fastest boats—which were built in abundance in the Detroit area—and police often had a hard time keeping up. Taken in April of 1931, this photo shows the Detroit Police and a portion of their river patrol arsenal during the last years of prohibition. The great cost of fighting smuggling, the loss of tax revenues, and the impossibility of preventing speakeasies (one estimate puts the number in Detroit alone at better than 25,000 in 1928), eventually swayed public and political support. Michigan was the first state to ratify the 18th amendment in 1933, thereby repealing prohibition.

Opposite, Bottom: An example of another kind of prohibition, this c. 1930 photo demonstrates how the sexes were divided on the bathing beaches. The sign at upper right reads "MEN NOT ALLOWED EAST OF THIS FENCE." Apparently women were allowed to mingle on the men's side, but men could not wander past the fence or the dock.

The construction of the new Belle Isle Bridge included reconfiguring the intersection of East Grand Boulevard and Jefferson, one of the busiest intersections in the city at the time. Pictured here is the excavation for a viaduct intended to allow the boulevard to bypass under Jefferson on its way to the new bridge, thereby alleviating traffic congestion at the intersection.

On November 1, 1923, the new Belle Isle Bridge, first named for George Washington, was opened with a parade of thousands led by the Detroit Police. At a final cost of $3 million, the modern bridge is more than 15 feet wider, for added lanes of traffic and broader sidewalks. Room was left for streetcar tracks, but they were not finished and streetcars never made it to the island. The bridge was later renamed for General Douglas MacArthur.

Looking north from Belle Isle across the new bridge, one can see the Grand Boulevard bypass of Jefferson, at the end of the bridge. This photo, from 1929, shows the old bus stop to the right of the viaduct and the great empty space to the right of the bridge where Electric Park used to reside. Still visible on the riverbank to the right of the bridge is the Detroit-side ferry dock, whose sign also advertises speed boat rides. With the construction of this new bridge large-vessel river traffic would now exclusively use the Canada-side channel. The wider four lane traffic of the new bridge was much better suited to provide ease of access to the park, whose visitors numbered in the tens of thousands per day at the time of this photograph.

This night photograph from the Detroit side of the river in 1931 looks across to the island and reveals, at lower left, that a ferry ride to the park cost 5¢, and a speedboat ride 50¢. Since buses traveled to the island with great regularity, at this time one would take a ferry for the novelty and fun.

Opened in 1924, the Detroit News Trail was exactly the kind of low-maintenance, nature-specific type of park feature that Olmsted envisioned park visitors would most enjoy. The trail went through the island's east-end woods, and could be taken on foot or on horseback.

The Detroit Yacht Club, founded in 1894, had become the city's preeminent social and recreational private club by the time this new clubhouse was constructed in 1923. The facility was built atop a man-made island that utilized fill dirt that was excavated from park and city construction projects, and was placed further east on Belle Isle to accommodate improvements on the island's public beaches. Opened the same year as the new bridge and many other improvements to the park, the clubhouse for the twelfth-oldest yacht club in the world solidified the organization's national and international renown with this elaborately tiled and paneled Spanish design. Though membership over the years has included some of the city's best-known and most affluent citizens, the club has also experienced the social and economic effects of time—suffering from flagging membership during the Depression and from the city's population drought of the 1960s and beyond. The DYC was, in fact, nearly evicted from its Belle Isle home in the 1960s over disputes about exclusive membership policies, and it was not until Detroit's African-American population was reaching a majority in the city that black members were allowed to join. Though not boasting the numbers it did in its heyday, membership in the early 21st century continues to be strong, and the DYC continues to be one of the island's most viable traditions.

For the 1901 City Bicentennial, city officials and dignitaries discussed the possibility of making a great memorial tribute statue to be placed at the far west end of the island. Potential subject for the memorial naturally included Cadillac and others of historic importance. A decision was not reached and the funds were never appropriated. When an irascible and combative gambler named James Scott left his entire fortune for a monument to himself in 1910, the city first recoiled at the source of the donation, but then went ahead with the project. Roughly 90 of the nation's leading architects submitted designs, and Cal Gilbert produced the winning entry. Pictured here is the unveiling event in 1925.

In addition to the fountain itself, a large lagoon that could be used for pleasure boating and gatherings of all kinds was created. Construction on the grounds began in 1916, and added 75 acres of territory to the island, consisting mostly of fill brought in from construction of the city's new skyscrapers. One of the nation's most elaborate fountains, it includes Pewabic Pottery artwork, is made with more than 10 tons of marble, and is one of Detroit's most recognizable symbols.

Opened in 1930, the Livingstone Lighthouse guides maritime traffic from Lake St. Clair into the Detroit River. The one-of-a-kind marble structure, designed by Albert Kahn, is named for a past Belle Isle Commissioner and a devoted shipping and maritime advocate who engineered a channel on the river to accommodate freighters. The filling in of the far west and east sides of the island added another one-half mile to the park's total length—bringing its present length to 2.5 miles. A 1940 WPA grant of $1.5 million paid for the landscaping of the area around the lighthouse.

Victor Kolar directed this summer concert on Belle Isle, June 30, 1936. Opened in the 1920s, this domed band shell was home to many musical events of both regional and national stature, until it fell into disrepair and was demolished in 1942.

78

From the Windsor side of the river, the skyline of 1928 Detroit is seen rising in the distance. The Penobscot building is just being finished, the Guardian is still in process and would be completed the next year. During the 1920s, Detroit construction placed third behind New York and Chicago, and only the economic devastation of the Great Depression could halt its upward movement. The Penobscot Building is 47 stories high, and was the tallest in the city until 1977.

Opposite, Top: There was a price to pay for the city's unfettered industrial, population, and economic growth. One of the reasons the people wanted Belle Isle for a park in the first place was that it had sold nearly all of its waterfront land for private and industrial use. Pictured here is a typical scene along the waterfront, where ships brought in mined and harvested materials that would be remade into construction materials for skyscrapers, homes, automobiles, and a great many other products. By the mid-20th century, Detroit was the number one manufacturing city in the world, and much of this industry was on or in close proximity to the Detroit River.

Opposite, Bottom: This aerial view was captured April 14, 1930. By this time, Detroit had reached its current geographical size—six times that of the turn of the 20th century. Its population then exceeded 1.5 million; it was the fourth largest city in the U.S. Between 1910 and 1930, the population of the city tripled. The photo is also a close approximation to what the skyline, looking up Woodward Avenue, looks like today.

The need for a large green space, where residents of the city could step back from their industrial lives, is evidenced in this aerial shot. The buildings and roads of Detroit, above the island, offset the thickness and darkness of the trees of the island. Downtown is to the left, and that's Grand River Avenue running away to the west. Visible here is the outline of the old island, now surrounded by additional fill that grew the park by nearly 300 acres in the 20th century.

Opened in 1929, just west of downtown, the Ambassador was the world's longest suspension bridge at the time. As its name suggests, the bridge was to be symbolic of a peaceful and welcoming relationship between nations. This scene shows the first people to cross over on opening day. A year later the Detroit-Windsor Tunnel also accessed downtown. Together the two would create the largest international crossing in North America.

The Nancy Brown Peace Carillon, built just before America's entrance into World War II, is situated between the band shell, the horticultural gardens, the Aquarium, and Lake Takoma. Paid for by readers of Brown's column in the *Detroit News*, the monument was built as a reminder of the many years of peace enjoyed between the U.S. and Canada.

The two shots on this page were taken on May 17, 1942 during the Coral Sea Victory Rally, which followed a large parade onto the island. The Peace Carillon rises in the right side of the photo. Later, a great cement and marble seating area that faces the carillon was built, where one can gaze across the river and ponder its engraving: "With Everlasting witness we keep Peace with our neighbors as they have kept peace with us throughout the years."

Also on May 17, 1942, Warren Bow speaks to a crowd on the island. Bow was the second President of another great Detroit institution, Wayne University (later Wayne State University), which trained hundreds of thousands for Detroit's war production effort, "The Arsenal of Democracy."

Looking more like a scene from a spaghetti western than from an urban law enforcement training photo, this is an image of Sergeant Swanter's Detroit Mounted Police of 1933. Belle Isle served as the training ground for these policemen, as did the Detroit River for other branches of the force and for the Navy, who operated a training facility at the foot of the Belle Isle Bridge.

There are several reasons given for Detroit's first race riot of the 20th century. One was the almost completely white police force in a city that had quickly become racially diverse due, especially, to African Americans who were recruited from the South to fuel the war effort in the factories. This is a shot of Hastings Street, in what was called the "Black Bottom"—a mostly black neighborhood on the city's near west side. For years, the black segment of the labor force received the hardest physical jobs (such as foundry work), and the lowest pay, and was segregated into ghettos, a situation that worsened during World War II.

The summer of 1943 was a hot one and Belle Isle was extremely crowded. On June 20, fights broke out on the island between blacks and whites, and more than 200 were arrested. Rumors soon began to circulate in the black community that whites had thrown a black woman and her baby off the Belle Isle Bridge, while in the white community the rumor was that blacks had raped and murdered a white woman at the same place. From either ends of downtown on Woodward, angry mobs of both races poured into the street. It was later thought the riot was exacerbated by the closing of the Belle Isle Bridge, which thereby deprived thousands of their usual place of comfort in summer.

With Belle Isle closed to the population, troops and the National Guard bivouacked on the island. President Roosevelt called in the reinforcements to put down the rioting, and the sight of the troops began to disperse the mobs. After 36 hours of rioting, 36 people were dead, the majority of them blacks who were beaten to death or shot by the police. Roughly 1,800 were arrested, also a majority black. Thurgood Marshall, later a Supreme Court Justice, called the riot "inevitable" because of the "weak-kneed policy of the Police Commissioner," and the "anti-Negro attitude of many members of the force."

These pictures date from the end of World War II. The Detroit River and Belle Isle were important training grounds for the Broadhead Naval Armory, located across the river from the island, and the Ford Naval Training Station.

Sailors here are on practice maneuvers for landing at Iwo Jima, a battle that proved important and decisive in the Pacific Theatre at the end of World War II. Pictured are amphibian tanks flanked by troops landing on the beaches of Belle Isle. Though the island was at one time used as a dueling ground for the city, nobody in Olmsted's time could have foreseen such military uses.

The 1950s saw an era of prosperity in the United States, but the city of Detroit was experiencing a time of great change. Manufacturing was beginning to move to the outlying suburbs of the city and the economic infrastructure of the once most industrious place in America was changing as well. Belle Isle would begin to adjust to shifts in economic support, as well, and the downsizing of its zoo facilities to a Children's Zoo in the mid-1950s was one of the first changes the island would face.

Still a thriving city of nearly two million people, in 1950, the new state-of-the-art Remick Band Shell was dedicated. Leonard B. Smith is seen here conducting the Detroit Concert Band under the stars, as he did often, to the delight of thousands. Music has always played an important role in the cultural health of the city, and the Remick Band Shell would host important outdoor concert events for many years.

The 1950s also marked the last of the ferry rides to Belle Isle. By the 1950s, the auto companies were producing approximately eight million cars per year, and in the Motor City, one drives. Seen here is the last ferry to carry passengers to the island, the *Belle Isle*, which could accommodate only 104 adults and 11 children—a small fraction of the numbers transported by the large pleasure steamers.

Also dedicated in 1950 was the new Skating Pavilion, named for William J. Flynn. Intended as a year-round facility, the new pavilion was to perform the same skate rental and other winter-time duties, while also serving refreshments and providing shelter in the warm weather months.

With the closing in of the second-story veranda half-finished, this photo from the winter of 1955 reveals changes to the historic Casino. At a time when the number of city visitors began to decline, the neon sign at the entrance advertises the Casino Cafeteria in order to better put in park seekers' money. Debates about commercial ventures on the island have persisted since the early days of the public park.

By the 1950s, the Horticulture Building (Conservatory) had fallen into disrepair. Built of wood, its ornate lattice and framework had deteriorated under the moist conditions and needed to be replaced. Anna Scripps Whitcomb was an enthusiastic orchid gardener with family ties to the Detroit News, and at the rededication—two years after her death and the will of her large orchid collection to the Conservatory—in 1955 the Conservatory was named in her honor.

The *J.T. Wing* was the last of the Great Lakes schooners. Brought to Belle Isle in 1945, the ship was dry-docked with the hope of transforming it into a historical museum. On the spot of what later would become the Dossin Great Lakes Museum, this photo dates from 1953, a year before it was burned because of dry rot.

After the *J.T. Wing* was burned because of dry rot, in 1956 the family of boating enthusiast Roy Dossin donated $125,000 to the Detroit Historical Commission for the construction of a new maritime museum. The Dossins also donated the new museum's first exhibit, the Gold Cup-winning *Miss Pepsi*—a longtime champion powerboat on the Detroit River. Detroit Council President Mary V. Beck, Robert Dossin, and Historical Commission President George Stark show off plans at the groundbreaking in 1959.

Made to be a register of the Great Lakes' rich maritime history, the Dossin features multiple scale models of important ships, as well as full-scale installations of the ornate Gothic Room from the steamer, the *City of Detroit III*, and the pilot house of the freighter, *William Clay Ford*. Visitors can "man the bridge" of the *Ford*, as if they were piloting a Great Lake freighter down the Detroit River.

During the Cold War, between 1955 and 1968, Belle Isle housed a Nike Air Defense System on its far east side, not far from the Livingstone Lighthouse. Because of the importance of Detroit's vast industry, it was long thought to be a target for long-range missiles. Once again the island would mirror the political and social issues of the day.

The insurrection of 1967 was a well-known and unfortunate moment for the city of Detroit. Known as the '67 Riot, it began on the near north side and quickly spread to all environs, though the downtown area was most affected. Once again, Belle Isle was involved when the thousands arrested could not fit into the city's jails and the men's bath house (at right) was used as a makeshift detention center. The bath house was never again used for its proper purpose, and was finally razed in the mid-1970s. The racial tensions exhibited in the riot, as well as the building of expressways and manufacturing outside the city, were two great reasons for the "white flight" that would devastate the population of Detroit. By the time of the census of 2000, the city's population would fall to less than one million—a figure not seen since the beginning of the automobile manufacturing explosion of the 1920s.

The Nature Center was opened in 1975, at a time when Americans were feeling a grassroots backlash to the country's industrial past and disregard for natural resources. Contributing to the community as an educational facility, the Center also performs research into the ecosystems and habitats of the metropolitan area. In the late 1990s, the endangered Pumpkin Ash and Shumand Oak trees were discovered in the old growth forest of the island's east end. Such research and outreach are important in providing stewardship and guidance for future ecological efforts. The construction of this facility also signifies a return to Olmsted's emphasis on the natural resources of a park, and the importance of its natural "genius."

Four

SEASONS
IN THE PARK

In this image, c. 1915, a family enjoys one of the great pleasures of the island park—watching the river and the constantly-changing panoramas it provides. Talk to anyone who visited Belle Isle in his or her youth, especially those old enough to have visited the island in its pristine heyday, and you will find that the park has a significant place in their memory. This unique place has provided stories to millions of visitors, and each will be as different as the time and year of their contact with it. Historically, it has been the commons of Detroit, and people interpret its past nostalgically.

This photo, taken March 8, 1938 shows the north shore between the Boat Club, the Detroit Yacht Club, and a frozen Detroit River. There's a tour bus headed toward the bridge, and one can see one of the island's many ice fountains (center), and the "Seven Sisters"—the smokestacks of a Detroit power-generating facility—on the horizon (top). Even in winter, the shorelines of the island are inviting.

During winter months one of the great attractions over the years has been the creation of ice fountains, some of them the size of houses if the weather has been cold for a long enough time.

Anyone for an open-air drive on a snow-covered island in the middle of a frozen river? Though it appears that this tour was chosen to leave the top down, there was a time when, if you wanted to take a ride in winter, you had no choice but to travel without the comfort of an enclosed vehicle. Cadillac was the first automaker to make enclosed cabs standard issue.

In 1894, a horse shelter was opened, and for many years the island had sleigh rental. The Dachshund pictured in this January 12, 1957 photo surely did not come with the rental of the sleigh.

Horses stabled on the island were used for many purposes. In this image dated January 193
horses pull felled lumber from the thick woods to the sawmill.

Skating was nearly as popular in winter as canoeing and swimming were in the summer
Belle Isle. These three young ladies are undaunted by Michigan winter, and so were hundre
of thousands of others.

The Skating Pavilion is on the left. Built as one of the early Victorian structures of the island, it rented skates, sold refreshments, and provided comfort until the Flynn Memorial was opened in 1950. The skating area extends along Lake Takoma, but skaters enjoyed exploring the connecting canals as well. In the 1990s public outdoor skating was moved to Hart Plaza, downtown, but there are plans for the restoration of the Flynn facility.

From February 15, 1942, this combined photo shows one of the many formal skating meets held on Lake Takoma. High schools throughout the metropolitan area held competitions on Belle Isle for Wayne County speed skating championships, and other events throughout the winter months.

This photo, from the Wayne Championships of 1934, shows a heat from the Senior Girls Race.

Another picture from the meet held on February 15, 1942, this image shows the start line from a heat of the men's finals. The Brown Peace Carillon can be seen at center.

Cars of the era completely line Lake Takoma for this winter scene in the late 1930s. Skaters are obviously aware of the photographer, falling down to get in the picture.

This photo was taken in the mid 1950s—at a time when the professional hockey club of Detroit, the Red Wings, dominated the sport and produced a great deal of community pride. A pair of skates, a stick, and a puck were all that were needed to play the game on Lake Takoma, unless you were stuck playing goalie, in which case you could play in street shoes (bottom left).

THE DETROIT BICYCLE BRIGADE AS IT APPEARS WHEN COMING ACROSS BELLE ISLE BRIDGE.

The arrival of spring for Detroiters, as for all midwestern cities, means coming outdoors after the winter. This front page article from Sunday morning, May 28, 1899, details the Detroit Bicycle Brigade's springtime crossing of the old Belle Isle Bridge. Even in the early days, cyclists were given their own trails and lanes of the roadways on the island.

Springtime also brought the first flower shows of the year to the conservatory, a world-class facility producing world-class events.

100

Players of the island's nine-hole golf course, opened in 1922, have enjoyed many a springtime round over the years. These ladies line up a putt on the eighth hole, right around the time the course was built.

Here's a foursome out to test the links on Opening Day of the season, April 13, 1928. The golf course has been used steadily since the time of its opening, and in the 1990s, island golf enthusiasts were treated to the opening of a driving range on the far east side of the park.

The spring of 1934 followed a winter of little snow and precipitation in the Detroit area producing low water levels in the canals and on the beaches of Belle Isle. Here beachcomber make the best of the situation, scavenging for treasures either washed up from the current c the river or lost from beachgoers of the summer months.

Spring on the island also brought about May Day celebrations, which attracted school childre from throughout the Detroit area. Parades and pageants were the order of the day on th occasion—a celebration of the arrival of summer. Children's Day, which took place in th summer, was also a great time of pageantry and congregation for the city's youth.

The island consistently played host to a number of large-scale special events over the years. This photo shows the volume of participants and amount of participation involved in creating these formally organized events. Belle Isle was the hub of such activity for the better part of the 20th century, and continues to host a wide range of community happenings.

Track and Field events for the metropolitan community and for the Detroit Public School System were also held on Belle Isle. Tens of thousands of participants and spectators would converge on the island for these events, held near the Athletic Pavilion (pictured at top). Pictured is the starting line for a track event, for which proper track attire and footwear must not have been mandatory (at right).

The fields of the Athletic Park held tennis courts, and later, soccer and football fields. This scene from 1927 shows the volume of school kids that participated and the variety of competitions waged. Signs in the photo refer to various trade events. Of note are the tents, at top, which demonstrate the duration of the competitions.

These Detroit Public School girls from June of 1928 are engaged in a match that measures stamina and agility—apparently keeping a ball in the air between either side of a suspended wire. Notice the athletic uniforms.

104

Fishing has always been a popular sport on the island and around the Detroit River area. For a number of years, an annual Fishing Derby was held on the island during the first week in June. Here, next to the Yacht Club, competitors tried their luck in 1965.

The art students pictured here take advantage of good summer weather and the early blooms of the season as they sketch and paint outside the Conservatory on June 30, 1949. The Conservatory was just about to undergo its restructuring.

It's hard to imagine a better way to ease the tension of city life other than drifting on the calm waters of the canals and lakes of Belle Isle. And the canals were used for more than recreation. In the early 20th century, they provided courting couples a socially acceptable place to be "alone."

"Getting away from it all" in the summer months, gliding along on placid waters under the willows of the island, one could possibly forget that a thriving industrial metropolis was a mile across the river.

A rowing team from the Detroit Boat Club places its shell into the river in 1928. Founded in 1839, the club has sponsored rowing teams each year since 1873, making it the longest continuously competing club in the United States. Though the facility is now closed, the DBC rows on.

Partly because of its protected position from the busy shipping channel that runs on the other side of the island, the Detroit side of the river is thought to be one of the best bodies of water for small craft boating in the United States. This photo shows the rowing team in competition during the 1920s. During its history, DBC rowing teams have won 54 events and 8 national championships.

Though the date of the photograph is unknown, these children are dressed in late 19th or early 20th century garb. Playgrounds on the island were some of its original equipment and were made in a rustic design. More durable steel frames later replaced the wooden structures.

Willow trees and the Detroit River provide a perfect backdrop for this extended family's picnic c. 1915. The primary weekend destination for an overwhelming number of Detroiters over the years, it was common to pack a complete lunch, or to cook one on the island in the warm weather months…and it still is. Again, notice the rustic picnic furniture.

This is an example of an early "boom box" on the island, c. 1920. Portable music has also long been a tradition for park goers. Perhaps not as portable as today's sound systems, Victrolas did come with suitcase-like carrying cases that could be packed up with lunch and taken in the car or on the trolley. With a Victrola, one would literally "crank the tunes."

Skimming stones and beachcombing are a popular pastime at the island's many waterfront vistas. The passage of ships and boats provide a constantly changing backdrop to activities on the island. These beachcombers were photographed in the 1920s.

Posing for the photographer, a young woman demonstrates her sleeping arrangements on Bell Isle during a heat wave in the summer of 1934. At a time when home air conditioning was novelty for the rich, the island offered some relief from the midwestern extremes of summer In early July of 1936, Detroit experienced a heat wave that took the lives of many, and sen hundreds of thousands to sleep in the open air of Belle Isle.

Undeterred by a street railways strike, this trio of comrades pedaled to Belle Isle in August of 1941. Though the city never laid tracks over the bridge to the island, streetcars were an important method of transportation to the island via Jefferson Avenue. Eventually replaced b buses, the last streetcar in Detroit ran in spring of 1956.

With yearly beach patronage on Belle Isle rising toward half a million in the 1920s, swimming safety became an increasing concern. Here a lifeguard takes a group of girls through swimming basics in the late 1910s. Water safety instruction, apparently, was just as segregated as the beaches.

This group of lifeguards protected swimmers at the men's beach. The badges present on the tops of some of the guards suggest their double duty as police officers.

Notwithstanding the rather artificial pose of this shot, the island provided elegant and natural panoramas for photographers from nearly every waterfront perspective. These bathing beauties were captured in the beach fashion of the day in front of the exclusive yacht club around 1928.

Those who didn't want to rent bathing suits at the bath house could always wade on shore in whatever version of a bathing suit they could produce. These children enjoy the cool waters of the river around 1910.

This social scene was photographed at the DYC in late June of 1934. In the background is the yacht "Nakomis," owned by automobile millionaire Horace B. Dodge. The yacht was at one time the largest on the great lakes at 243 feet in length.

This is a typically busy men's bathing beach in the 1920s, before formal diving piers were constructed. Although men were not allowed on the women's beach, women were allowed to visit the men's. It was not until the mid-1930s that men were allowed to go bare above the waist on the public beach.

Though segregation continued to be the norm in Detroit, in this photo we witness a joining of both race and sex on the bathing beach in June of 1949.

The bathing beach could be used for more than swimming. Beauty pageants were popular events on the island. This group of amateur contestants paraded for a crowd of well-dressed onlookers around 1915.

These bathers sit on a breakwater at the boundary of the swimming area in the 1920s. There are a number of anachronisms in the dress of these women. As is evident from the previous photograph, swimsuits of the "Roaring Twenties" were, for one, shorter and less conservative than those in this photo. As well, it was not customary (nor particularly safe) to wear stockings and shoes in the water at this time.

More in fashion for the day, these beauty contestants pose on the grand marble sculpture of Scott Fountain in September of 1929. To get the most out of the last warm weather of the season, the end of summer brought many special events to Belle Isle.

Neptune, and his somewhat bemused-looking mermaids, arrives for the festivities of the Water Carnival at the end of the water sports season in 1929. The Water Carnival was a great annual event for many years, as were many other special events sponsored by the Boat and Yacht Clubs

Competitions of all kinds—both traditional and unconventional—were the flavor of the Water Carnival. This photo, from 1926, shows a traditional diving competition.

These next two photos, both from 1929, show some of the more unconventional competitions of the Water Carnival. This shot demonstrates the two-man canoe joust aboard vessels that were normally used for much more peaceful activities on the island's canals.

Another Water Carnival competition was the pillow fight, where the contestants would sit atop a ship mast or flagpole and try to knock each other into the river. Notice the "Belle Isle" pillow—which could be rented with a canoe—used by the contestant at left, and the decorative wainscoting on the diving board at top.

These two photographs, also from 1929, feature boat races at the Water Carnival. The water sports season ended with the biggest outdoor event of the year—the hydroplane races on the Detroit River—and these races between members of the Yacht and Boat Clubs were something of a warm-up for those events. In this first photo is a regatta.

By the affiliation flags on the bows of these yachts we know this race is between members of the Detroit Yacht Club. Competitions of this sort have been an important part of the social calendar of the DYC since its beginning, though summer is not the only time when the club hosts social events. Notice the vintage wooden boats, an important part of Detroit River culture to this day.

Also known as "The Silver Fox" and "King Gar," Gar Wood was the first superstar of boat racing. From 1917 until 1933, he completely dominated APBA Gold Cup and Harmsworth unlimited events on the Detroit River. An industrialist and master inventor from Wisconsin, his average speed in the multi-engine *Miss America* in a 30-mile race in 1920 was 70 miles per hour—a record that would stand in its class until 1946. After Wood's appearance on the scene, the rules had to be changed. Detroit was to become a leader in the manufacture of boat engines, and the city embraced Wood as its own. He was the first Commodore of the Detroit Yacht Club when it opened its new facility in 1923.

This photograph is Gar Wood taking the checkered flag aboard *Miss America I* in 1921. With this boat, Wood won the Harmsworth in England in 1920, and after winning, brought the race to the Detroit River the following year for the first time. He won Detroit's first Harmsworth that next year, as well as the APBA Gold Cup.

Here's Wood again aboard *Miss America V*. Wood was the winner of the Harmsworth aboard this boat in 1926, with an average speed of 61 miles per hour. This was Wood's third consecutive victory of six. He lost the race only once between 1920 and 1933—to his brother George in 1931. By this time, and because of Wood, the Harmsworth had become a permanent fixture of late summers on the Detroit River, and would remain so until the late 1950s.

Here's a good picture of the awesome power Wood harnessed to drive his boats. This is *Miss America VI*, equipped with twin made-in-Detroit Packard engines, and requiring two on-board mechanics to tend to the motors during a race. The motors are largely unmuffled, and could be heard for miles. Later in the 20th century Belle Isle would play host to another kind of motor racing, this time on wheels—the Gran Prix.

This photo provides a good impression of what it's like to watch the race from the Yacht Club. Just about any surface that can hold a spectator is occupied, and the river is jammed with anchored boats as well. The race here is between *Miss America VII* and *VIII*. *Miss America VII* won the Harmsworth in 1926, *VIII* in 1927.

John Hacker, aboard one of his HackerCraft models, is seen here speeding past the Yacht Club in 1929. Famous for the "V bottom design," Hacker founded his boat-making business in Detroit in 1914 at 323 Crane Avenue. His most famous boats, from the 1920s, were mahogany models called "Belle Isle Bear Cats," and were popular with prominent Detroit dignitaries like Edsel Ford and J.W. Packard.

Here's a shot of My Sweetie, a hydroplane designed by John Hacker. Though Hacker was a consistent victor in the 1930s, his victories in the big races came mostly outside of Detroit. My Sweetie, though, was the winner of the APBA Gold Cup on the Detroit River in 1949.

As is obvious from the crowd shots of the hydroplane races, Detroiters have a great and historical love of these late-summer spectaculars on the river. Part of the reason for the popularity of the events is that they are visible from a multitude of places on the river, and there is no charge. Over the years, entrepreneurs have found ways to charge for grandstand seating on the Detroit side of the river, but the vantage point of the public beaches of Belle Isle remains free and is one of the best.

This photo, from 1938, shows the international interest in Detroit hydroplane racing. Capturing the Gold Cup here is *Alagi*, an Italian boat owned and driven by Count Theo Rossi—the first to capture the top award from outside North America. Detroit hydroplane enthusiasts will regale interested parties with their favorite racers and boats—from Guy Lombardo to Bill Muncie—and folklore of the sport is to some as important as that of the automobile.

The late blooms of the horticultural gardens also come at the end of summer. World-class gardeners and their teams work all year to produce the exotic and indigenous species grown in the beds around the Conservatory. This photo shows the extensive dahlia garden in September of 1946.

As bulbs are being arranged and planted for the next spring in the horticultural gardens, the Conservatory is signaling the arrival of fall with its annual Mum Show. Barely visible in the middle of this photo is a well-scented exhibition-goer amidst the enormous blossoms.

When the trees began to turn and the crowds began to thin fishing was particularly good on the island's canals. At one time, the canals were opened to the Detroit River, and were therefore stocked with natural habitation fish. This boy has a can of worms and a homemade pole to try his luck the old fashioned way, *c.* 1940s.

Another peaceful and bucolic fishing scene, this one takes place by the old canoe rental. Fishing is a very popular pastime in the city of Detroit, whether by boat or on the banks of the river, and fall is the time to catch migratory species.

Fall, to the metropolitan area's younger community, has always meant going back to school. For the young men in these next two photos, school means "college," and of course college doesn't always involve books. The College of the City of Detroit for many years held its "rush" activities on Belle Isle, which involved many games and feats of strength. Here a freshman class involves itself in a traditional tug of war; the team pictured is obviously on the losing end at this moment.

Another CCD rush activity, another feat of team strength—this one involves pushing giant ball over a goal line. With the arrival of winter, the park is used less by groups than b individuals seeking solitary peace and quiet in a simple jog, bike ride, or drive around the park natural and constructed wonders.

Anyone who has spent a full year of seasons in the Midwest knows the mixture of beauty and apprehension that is brought on with the coming of fall. The leaves produce spectacular and colorful scenery, though the wise know that it is not without a price—winter will not be long to follow. Because of its natural beauty, Belle Isle has long been a destination for those who wish to embrace this reflective time of the year—to ponder the past and question the present and the future.

Belle Isle has long and often been in this metaphorical position, with which the City of Detroit looks fondly on the park's past, but goes with trepidation into the park's future. Though still a thriving recreational park, the infrastructure of the island decays without the necessary support. There is a Proposed Master Plan for Belle Isle which attempts to identify primary areas of need, and your interest and backing could be helpful. If you can help, please contact one of the following organizations: Friends of Belle Isle, Greening of Detroit, Belle Isle Nature Center, Cityscape Detroit, City of Detroit Recreation Department, Belle Isle Botanical Society, or Friends of the Detroit River.

Bibliography

Anderson, Janet (2001). *Island in the City: How Belle Isle Changed Detroit Forever*. Detroit: Friends of Belle Isle.

Angelo, Frank. *Yesterday's Detroit* (1974). Miami: E. A. Seemann.

Beveridge, Charles F. and Hoffman, Carolyn F. (1997). *The Papers of Frederick Law Olmsted*, supplementary series, vol 1. Baltimore and London: Johns Hopkins.

Burton, Clarence (1922). *The City of Detroit Michigan 1701–1922*, vol. 5. Detroit-Chicago: Clarke.

Commissioners of Parks and Boulevards of the City of Detroit (1899). *Souvenir, American Park and Outdoor Art Association, June 27–29, 1899*. [Detroit]

Detroit News (2000). Rearview Mirror. Retrieved 2001 from: http://pc99.detnews.com/history/archive.hbs

Detroit Yacht Club (2001). *Watermark II, 2001*. Detroit: Detroit Yacht Club.

Dunnigan, Brian Leigh (2001). *Frontier Metropolis: Picturing Early Detroit, 1701–1838*. Detroit: Wayne State.

Farmer, Silas (1969). *History of Detroit and Wayne County and Early Michigan*, 3rd ed. Detroit: Gale.
Ferry, Hawkins W (1987). *The Legacy of Albert Kahn*. Detroit: Wayne State.

Holli, Melvin G., and Jones, Peter d'A (1981). *Biographical Dictionary of American Mayors, 1820–1980*. Westport, Conn.: Greenwood.

Hydroplane History (1999). Retrieved 2002 from: http://www.lesliefield.com/Default.htm

Keep, Helen E. (1916). *Guide to Detroit*. Detroit: Detroit News.

Mason, Philip (1995). *Rumrunning and the Roaring Twenties*. Detroit: Wayne State University.

Olmsted, Frederick Law (1883). *The Park for Detroit: Being a Primary Consideration of Certain Prime Conditions of Economy for Belle Isle Scheme*. Detroit: Richmond, Bachus & Co.

Oxford, William (1992). *The Ferry Steamers*. Erin, Ontario: Boston Mills.

Planning research organization for a better environment (1973). *Historic Belle Isle: Application for National Register of Historic Places*. Unpublished manuscript: PROBE.

Poremba, David Lee (2001). *Detroit in its World Setting: A Three Hundred Year Chronology, 1701–2001*. Detroit: Wayne State University.

Widick, B.J. (1972). *Detroit: City of Race and Class Violence*. Chicago: Quadrangle.